O! WHAT A DAY!

Written and Illustrated by Oliver Bestul

"...to room 23."

Published by Orange Hat Publishing 2016

ISBN 978-1-943331-25-3

Copyrighted © 2016 by Oliver Bestul

All Rights Reserved

O! WHAT A DAY!

Written and Illustrated by Oliver Bestul

Proudly printed in the United States of America

Orange Hat
PUBLISHING

www.orangehatpublishing.com
Waukesha, WI

OLIVER OSTRICH was nervous one morning,
for it was his first day of school.
He knew not the names of the kids in his class,
nor had he memorized the rules.

With a chattering beak and sweaty palm-feathers,
he went nearer the door to room 23.

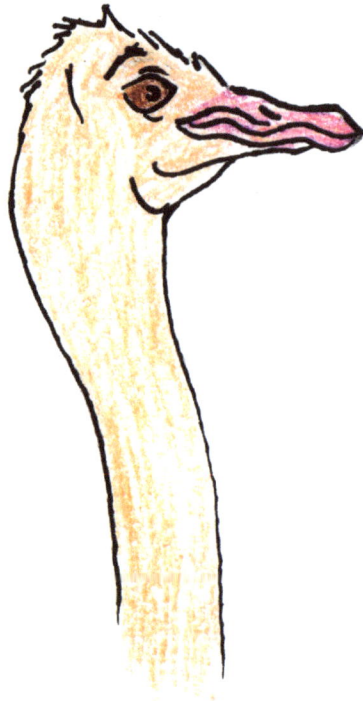

It swung in suddenly, and with the widest of grins
there stood **MRS. CLAY CHIMPANZEE**.

"Welcome," Mrs. Clay said, "to my wonderful class.
You're sure to have a howling good time.
I can introduce you to the kids if you'd like."
Oliver nodded shyly in reply.

"Well, that pair over there are as kind as they come.
In their helpfulness they are akin."
With a meek little squawk, Oliver asked them their names.
"GRACE GAZELLE." "And I'm PIPER PENGUIN."

"And those boys in the corner," continued Mrs. Clay,
"nearly hidden behind their book fort,
well, that's **SEAMUS SUGAR GLIDER** and **MARLEY MEERKAT**.
Go to them when you write a report."

"You don't have to introduce me to all of the kids,"
Oliver said, braver now than before.
"If it's alright with you, Mrs. Clay," he went on,
"I myself can see what is in store."

The next duo he met brought Oliver joy,
as math was something he adored.
BRADY BABOON, **ROWAN RAM**, and he
multiplied using a checkerboard.

Multiplication was over, now on to division.
Both **MADDUX MOOSE** and **JAMES JUNGLE CAT**
taught Oliver how to put pegs in a board
to visualize the answers they arrived at.

Then **LEO THE LION** declared it his turn
to teach Oliver Ostrich a thing or two.
He helped his new friend memorize all the vowels.
"A, E, I, O," Leo roared, "and don't forget U!"

And drawing a picture while deep in her thoughts
sat the soft-spoken **MISS ROSE RACCOON**.
Oliver learned, upon talking with her,
quiet creatures speak beautifully when opportune.

ANDERSON ALLIGATOR had a kind enough heart
to let Oliver read with him out of his book.
They sounded out a story of a cat on a bus
and all the adventures the character took.

Now **ARCELIA ARMADILLO** and **MACKENZIE MOUSE**,
along with their friend **VIOLET VAMPIRE BAT**,
showed Oliver a metal that stuck to most others
and called the hickeydoo a magnet.

$\frac{1}{8}$ $\frac{1}{10}$ $\frac{1}{3}$

$\frac{1}{5}$ $\frac{1}{12}$ $\frac{1}{4}$

Later **JACOB THE JAY** took Oliver aside,
for he knew it was time to take action.
He simply could not let a companion go
without having learned all the fractions!

During lunch, Oliver found himself sitting between
LEAH LEMUR and **ABIGAIL AARDVARK**.
They both had him laughing throughout the whole meal
making faces and witty remarks.

Out at recess, at all of the boys' request,
Oliver joined in a game of football.
LOGAN LEOPARD guarded **JOSEPH JACKAL**.
HENRY HEDGEHOG was covered as well.

It was by a stroke of luck that Oliver saw
a spot where the defense had broken.
He let the ball fly, and to his surprise
the catch was made by **LOBSTER LOGAN**!

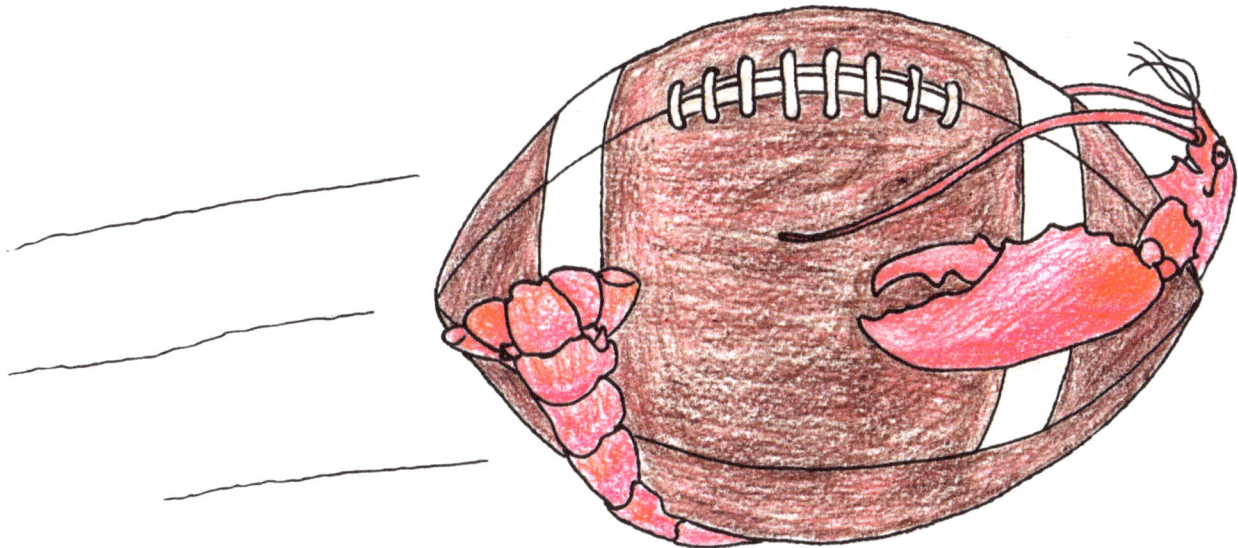

Back in the indoors, Oliver joined in a game
to get four of his chips in a line.
ZACHARY ZEBRA, **FRANK FOX**, and **KIARA KANGAROO**
all played to the end, a four-way tie.

RISHAV RHINO then challenged the ostrich
to a battle of wits in the form of chess.
The two-horned mammal proved to him in minutes
that at this game he was the best.

Next, Oliver was called over by two new faces,
WREN WOODPECKER and **LILY LADYBUG**.
These two girls were clear masters of speedy addition,
so all he could do was stand there and shrug.

RITA RABBIT then asked him, "Oh, what is the hour?"
unaware Oliver couldn't tell time.
So with **VIOLET VULTURE** and **STAR SNOWY OWL**,
she brought the bird up to a clock-reading prime.

5-1=4
9×5=45
4+5=9

8-1=7
9×8=72
7+2=9

7-1=6
9×7=63
6+3=9

Oliver learned another math trick
from **NETTIE NARWHAL**, who lived near the marina.
She taught him to multiply numbers by nine
with much help from friend **HEDY HYENA**.

Sooner than Oliver ever imagined,
Mrs. Clay Chimpanzee said, "The school day now ends."
He could hardly wait for the following day . . .

. . .when he'd see all his new friends again.

Rita   Piper   Zoe

Will   Grace   Anderson

Lily   Indy   Rose

Abby   Seah   marley

Violet p

Rishav   Logan & Kiara   Logan

Holly   Henry

Pearl   Brody   Seamus

nettie   James   Kennedie

Lea

Rowan   Violet B

Jacob   Maddux

Star   Thank You!
        Ms. Clay

www.ingramcontent.com/pod-product-compliance
Lightning Source LLC
Chambersburg PA
CBHW040232070426
42447CB00030B/157